BUILDING
MANHATTAN

BY **LAURA VILA**

VIKING

VIKING

Published by Penguin Group

Penguin Young Readers Group, 345 Hudson Street, New York, New York 10014, U.S.A.

Penguin Group (Canada), 90 Eglinton Avenue East, Suite 700, Toronto, Ontario, Canada M4P 2Y3

(a division of Pearson Penguin Canada Inc.)

Penguin Books Ltd, Registered Offices: 80 Strand, London WC2R 0RL, England

First published in 2008 by Viking, a division of Penguin Young Readers Group

1 3 5 7 9 10 8 6 4 2

LIBRARY OF CONGRESS CATALOGING-IN-PUBLICATION DATA

Vila, Laura.

Building Manhattan / by Laura Vila.

p. cm.

ISBN 978-0-670-06284-3 (hardcover)

1. Manhattan (New York, N.Y.)—History—Juvenile literature.

2. New York (N.Y.)—History—Juvenile literature. I. Title.

F128.33.V55 2008

974.7'1—dc22

2007038119

Manufactured in China

Set in Blue Highway

Book design by Nancy Brennan

To the Islanders—L.V.

LONG AGO, before maps or words were used,

a little island formed.

Tall grasses and small animals lived on its shores.

Then came birds, possums, and raccoons to live in its woods.

The first people came and built homes using sticks and bark.

They lived with the land—hunting, gathering, and planting crops.

The Dutch came searching for land and riches.

They made maps of every place they explored.

The Dutch traded fur and cut down timber.

They built a fort and a windmill on the land they cleared.

The English sailed across the Atlantic, too.

Many brought their families to start new lives.

These settlers built a colony,

and then a nation where new freedoms grew.

Boats and boats packed with people, traditions,

languages, and new ideas clogged the shores.

These people built skinny row houses

on skinny roads with funny names.

Crossing wide waters with iron and steel,

engineers built great bridges.

Automobiles, planes, and trains brought more people.

Some were just visiting, and others chose to stay.

With steel they built skyscrapers

over one hundred stories high.

People came to see the sights, take pictures,

and share the city with the rest of the world.

It grew and it grew

and people still come.

The building of Manhattan is never done.

TIME LINE

50,000–11,000 B.C.E.

Manhattan is an island. It is thirteen miles long and about two miles wide. It is covered with sprawling meadows and woodlands. Its waters are home to fish, oysters, seals, and porpoises.

1500 B.C.E.–1600 C.E.

The Lenape people are the first to live on Manhattan. They live in harmony with the land and build homes and structures that do not change the landscape.

1609

Henry Hudson explores the rivers surrounding Manhattan on behalf of the Dutch East India Company. He is searching for a route through the Americas to Asia.

1614

The Dutch establish a trading post on the southern tip of Manhattan, which develops into the settlement of New Amsterdam by 1624. The Dutch merchants' main business is fur trading with the Lenape people.

1667

The Dutch turn over New Amsterdam to the British as a result of a war treaty. The British rename New Amsterdam New York.

1776

The United States declares independence from Britain. In 1789 the Constitution is ratified and George Washington is elected president. He lives at 1 Cherry Street in lower Manhattan.

1800–1900

A great migration brings more than thirty million people to the U.S. through Manhattan. This wave of immigrants is largely Irish, German, Russian, and Italian.

1850–1950

Immigrants fill Manhattan, and neighborhoods are established based on common cultural beliefs and languages. Evidence of this can be seen today in cultural pockets like Little Italy and Chinatown.

1909

The Manhattan Bridge, a two-level suspension bridge, is built between Canal Street in Manhattan and Flatbush Avenue in Brooklyn. The bridge is 6,855 feet long.

1940s

Automobiles rise in popularity and Americans begin to travel greater distances. Manhattan becomes a premiere tourist destination.

1950–1970

Advances in building methods and materials make it possible to build ever-taller skyscrapers. By 1970, buildings are taller and larger than they've ever been.

1970 to the Present

Tourism is an important industry to Manhattan. In 1971 the city officially adopted the nickname the Big Apple. Approximately forty million people visit New York City every year.

In the Future

Many civilizations and cultures have lived on—and loved—Manhattan. It is constantly growing and changing, and its future will be built upon the ideas and efforts of everyone who calls this island home.

BIBLIOGRAPHY

Jackson, Kenneth. *The Encyclopedia of New York*. New Haven: Yale University Press, 1995.

Lightfoot, Fredrick, and Josephine Johnson. *Maritime New York in Nineteenth-Century Photographs*. New York: Dover Publications, 1980.

Milton, Giles. *Nathaniel's Nutmeg*. New York: Penguin Books, 2000.

Pritchard, Evan. *Native New Yorkers*. San Francisco/Tulsa: Council Oak Books, 2002.